TWELVE LOOPS

TWELVE LOOPS
A System of Poems Without Metaphor

by J. A. Gucci

Teacher Edition

Poetic structure through paradox, repetition, and physical form.

Twelve short poems rooted in observable systems —designed for high school analysis, discussion, and creative response.

Pressure System Press

New York, New York

2026

**Twelve Loops: Poems Without Metaphor
(Teacher Edition)**
© 2026 J. A. Gucci
Published by Pressure System Publishing

All rights reserved.
No part of this publication may be reproduced or transmitted in any form or by any means, electronic or mechanical, without permission in writing from the publisher, except for brief quotations used in reviews or educational settings.

Printed in the United States of America

ISBN: 979-8-9946751-2-0

www.jagucci.com

Table of Contents

Acknowledgments 7

Potoo Bird Breathing Loop
Voice / Self / Silence 9

Glacial Milk and Mist
Time / Moment / Eternity 11

Salt Flat and the Cactus
Matter / Mind / Being 13

Lake Reflection, Distortion
Image / Body / Absence 15

Word on Clay, Rift Echo
Word / Pattern / Break 17

Binary Code, Evolution, Glitch
Rule / Error / Form 19

Whisper Gallery
Signal / Interruption / Memory 23

Bee Sting, Still Curl
Obedience / Reflex / Sacrifice 25

Bark Explosion, Crown Shyness
Sacrifice / Limit / Grace 27

Summit That Isn't
Desire / Distance / End 29

Octopus Shifts Shape
Imitation / Echo / Transformation 31

Coffee Stirring Loop
Return / Trace / Begin 33

Classroom Guide.................... 35

Acknowledgments

I thank the high school band students I've taught over the years for allowing poetry to enter a room built for sound. This book is for those who weren't afraid to change tempo, form, or change tools.

Triad Teaching Note

Voice / Self / Silence

(Potoo Bird Breathing Loop)

This poem presents a still, nocturnal landscape where motion is minimal but pressure is present. The bird's looped breath system, predator-prey tension, and camouflage behavior are all real—not metaphor. "One-way loop" is not symbolic: it names an irreversible physical condition.

Prompt:

What is the role of stillness in this poem? What patterns create silence without using the word "quiet"?

Potoo Bird Breathing Loop

One-way loop,
shut eye.

Undulating branch—
steady,

snapped—
guttural shriek,

still mouse twitching—
silent crickets.

Gray night-liver—
owl gaze.

Triad Teaching Note

Time / Moment / Eternity
(Glacial Milk and Mist)

The poem follows the literal water cycle: glacier to stream to ocean to mist. The loop is continuous but irreversible—once the drop falls, it doesn't return the same. The paradox lies in how an eternal system is built from single, unrecoverable moments. "Drop" and "cascade" both function as noun and verb—hinges of motion and consequence.

Prompt:
How does this poem show change without describing transformation? What makes the cycle feel both permanent and unstable?

Glacial Milk and Mist

Glacial milk,
meandering stream—
cascade:

fresh water
fall—

salty ocean—
mist.

Triad Teaching Note

Matter / Mind / Being
(Salar de Uyuni, the Man and the Cactus)

Set in the Bolivian salt flats, this poem uses geological and atmospheric elements—steam vents, salt pools, cactus islands—to present a real environment.

A human action enters the system ("I croon"), introducing a response that does not alter the physical conditions but changes how the environment is engaged.

The landscape remains physically stable; the interaction introduces variation within it.

Prompt:
What happens when a mind projects onto a place? Is this poem describing reality or reacting to it?

Salt Flat and the Cactus

Purple clouds drift
across the crusting ground—
water glaze.

Splayed—
pink pool
wooly cactus bloom—
I croon.

Steaming mud pots—
rock pilla

Triad Teaching Note

Image / Body / Absence

(Lake Reflection and Distortion)

The poem begins in a mirror: spruce and fir trees appear beautiful and symmetrical in the lake's surface. But the reflection is unstable—wind, scent, and growth patterns disrupt the illusion. The reader is invited to compare what's seen with what is. The final word, "ripples," is both event and erasure.

Prompt:

What is real in this poem: the reflection or the distortion? How does absence reveal itself through form?

Lake Reflection, Distortion

Teal toothed—
ragged spruce,
isosceles indigo—
fluted fir.

Bark beetle bores a hole—
turpentine air,
flitting crossbill—
puffed.

Glass lake—
natant needle—
ripples.

Triad Teaching Note

Word / Pattern / Break

(Rift Valley, Voice as Mark)

This poem breaks sound into fragments—croaks, growls, a screech—and links them to physical spaces. The central "word" is not language but impact: scraped on clay, uttered once, then lost. The setting is prehistoric and contemporary at once. The paradox: pattern is hinted at, but never formed.

Prompt:

How does this poem treat language as physical? What is the relationship between voice and environment?

Word on Clay, Rift Echo

Croaks in a rift valley,
desert growls,
screech—

. . .

word—
scraped on clay,
uttered—

gasp—
in the grassland.

Triad Teaching Note

Rule / Error / Form

(Binary, Pattern, Evolution)

This poem builds from the raw material of code: 0s and 1s repeat, glitch, and restructure into new forms. It begins with certainty ("0 / 1") and ends with mutation. The paradox is that form emerges from failure—errors are not flaws, but generative forces. "Render— / become" marks the moment when information turns into identity.

Prompt:

How do patterns change when they repeat? Where does structure end and transformation begin?

Binary Code, Evolution, Glitch

0
1

This—
that.

01

This—
and that:

Awareness.

. . .

01
01

0101

pAtTeRn/ErOrR
TIME / change.

. . .

01101
01
000
01

Information:
reality.

E. v. o. l. U. T. I. O. N.

. . .

Exchange:
repeat:
exchange:
repeat:

render—
become.

Triad Teaching Note

Signal / Interruption / Memory

(Whispering Gallery, Fragmented Voice)

A whisper crosses a chamber but is blocked mid-transit—broken by a pillar. What reaches the listener is incomplete. The structure is based on the real acoustics of Grand Central Station, where signals must be reassembled by memory. The poem shows how communication becomes a partnership: one sends, the other reconstructs.

Prompt:

What does the poem suggest about shared meaning? Where does memory act as the author?

Whisper Gallery

A whisper—
clung to jagged limestone

scattered—
blocked by a pillar—

secret.

Triad Teaching Note

Obedience / Reflex / Sacrifice

(Bee Sting, Hive Defense)

A hand meets a hive, and the bee responds—not with choice, but with reflex. The poem is tightly physical: the stylet and lancet (real anatomical terms) describe a process that ends in death. There's no metaphor—just consequence. The stillness at the end ("still curl") is not poetic repose; it is factual and final.

Prompt:

Where in this poem is obedience? What is sacrificed, and is it conscious?

Bee Sting, Still Curl

Stylet and lancet
rammed into hide.

Tattering wings—
twitching—

still curl.

Triad Teaching Note

Sacrifice / Limit / Grace

(Exploding Bark and Crown Shyness)

This poem begins in winter: sap expands and bark bursts under pressure. What follows is seasonal biology—dead leaves contribute to new growth, and tree crowns develop with visible gaps between them (crown shyness).

Growth occurs through spacing and limitation. The system organizes itself without overlap, producing a structured pattern of separation.

Prompt:

How does the tree's loss become part of its structure? What does the poem suggest about restraint as growth?

Bark Explosion, Crown Shyness

Splattered rainbows
elongated shadows,

a trunk—
explodes.

Dead leaves,
hissing wind—

Spring—
shy crown.

Triad Teaching Note

Desire / Distance / End

(Summit That Isn't)

The climber reaches what appears to be the end—sky bent, breath gone, peak beneath him—only to find the mountain continues. The poem resists reward. "Bent indigo skies" is not abstraction but a literal description of high-altitude optics. The final line—a mountain—is not metaphor. It's the absurd truth of ambition: you get there, and it goes on.

Prompt:

What does the poem deny the speaker? What kind of ending is offered instead?

Summit That Isn't

A crampon
rammed into ice,
rock—

lift,
heave,
breathless—

bent indigo skies,
a peak—

mid-slope.

Triad Teaching Note

Imitation / Echo / Transformation
(Octopus Shifts Shape)

The octopus does not speak—it becomes. The poem catalogs its changes: black and yellow arms (mimicking danger), red-brown (camouflage), then slate gray (return). Each stage is literal, observable, and tactical. Imitation is not expression—it's survival. Transformation comes only after echoing fails.

Prompt:
How does the octopus "speak" in this poem? What's the difference between changing and becoming?

Octopus Shifts Shape

Black and yellow arms—
undulating,

splayed—
red-brown,

pulled together—
slate grey,

Flat,
lion fish—
octopus.

Triad Teaching Note

Return / Trace / Begin

(Coffee Stirring Loop)

This poem begins and ends in a cup—but nothing resets. The stirring motion loops forward and backward, but the mixture never separates. Time appears reversible; change is not. "Rapid right circles" and "laving left loops" describe mirrored motion, but the tan and bronze remain—evidence of a transformation that cannot be undone.

Prompt:

What does this poem say about cause and effect? Can motion repeat if the state has changed?

Coffee Stirring Loop

Black topped
shimmering crema—
cream—

plunged deep,
billow back—
I stir:

rapid right circles,
laving left loops—

tan,
bronze.

Classroom Use Guide

Teaching Twelve Loops in the Secondary Classroom

This book is a system—not a collection. Each poem is constructed from literal, observable realities, without metaphor, narrative, or expressive confession. The goal is not to interpret a speaker's intention, but to **trace how language behaves under pressure**—through paradox, precision, and form.

How to Use This Book

- Assign one poem per week, paired with the triad
- Treat each as a **close reading object**—brief, durable, rich in structure
- Use the **Teaching Notes** in the back as post-reading scaffolds, not guides
- Begin by reading aloud, twice. Then silently. Then visually (on screen or board)

What Students Learn

- How to analyze poetry that resists symbolism
- How language performs rather than explains
- How observation, repetition, and pressure create form
- How systems can mean without stories

Suggested Activities

1. **No Metaphor Mondays**
   - Read a poem aloud. Students list all observable actions and transformations.
   - No speculation. Only traceable facts.

2. **Triad Mapping**
   - Have students map each triad onto the poem using color-coded annotations.

3. **Reverse Reading**
   - Begin with the final image. Ask: what physical process led here?

4. **Expressive Thirds Analysis**
   - Break poem into: Sensory / Conceptual / Ontological.
   - Ask: what happens in each orbit?

5. **Compression Lab**
   - Students write a poem using only 30 words to describe a real process or system—no metaphor, no commentary.

Where It Fits

Suitable for:

- AP Literature: form, tone, ambiguity
- Honors English: compression, syntax
- Creative Writing: structure, constraint
- General English: close reading, scientific language in literary form

Composition Prompts

Student Writing in the System

These exercises are designed to help students create original work **within the same constraints** as Twelve Loops. Each prompt guides them to build poetry rooted in **observable systems, non-metaphorical language,** and **structured paradox.**

Prompt 1: The System Poem

Write a poem that traces a real system—biological, mechanical, environmental, or social.
You may not use metaphor or symbol. Only literal, observable steps.

Your goal:

- Use **sensory detail** (sight, sound, motion)
- Highlight a **process that transforms** something over time
- Include a paradox (e.g. "irreversible change from reversible motion")

Length: 12–20 lines
Title: Use a triad of concepts (e.g. "Signal / Gap / Completion")

Prompt 2: The Triad Response

Choose one triad from the book.
Write a poem that embodies that paradox—without narrative, commentary, or emotional expression.

Example:

Triad: Desire / Distance / End
You could write about: an echo across a canyon, a bee returning to a vanished flower, or a signal traveling through space.

Constraints:

- No figurative language
- Use only what can be heard, seen, touched, or traced
- Let form do the speaking

Prompt 3: Echo Loop

Begin with a real event or object (e.g. a light turning on, a drain swirling, a cicada emerging).
Describe it as a **loop** that does not return.
Use only physical terms. Let the structure reveal the contradiction.

Try to end the poem on a word that opens the cycle again.

Each of these can be copied, printed, or projected in class.
Students should revise with an eye toward:

- Compression
- Clarity
- Structural resonance (the feeling of something inevitable)